HECTIC PIGMENT

Jed Rasula

OPO
books & objects

Opo Books & Objects
abadpennyreview.com

Hectic Pigment

ISBN: 978-0-9973048-2-4

Library of Congress
Control Number: 2017905643

In memory of DQ, "Mister Dog"

HECTIC PIGMENT

Table of Contents

Giacometti's Dog

—applications *of, from, & as*

I'll tell you this much:
space is pierced with a bony flicker

a woman on the street sold me a spinal column
so I put it on, I put it *in*

for years I crawled around
in a rubble of numbers
a palace of matchsticks
was all I could muster

outside my cage
everything happens
just before daybreak
a skeleton twitters
wrinkles a puddle
flapping its featherless wings

there may be nothing there
but pointless points
dripping
nothing but sizzle & chatter
but the bones won't stop
baring themselves
to all & sundry alike.

(What does *sundry* mean?)

Finally, one day, a statue became a needle.

". . . and I was *that dog*."

a gaunt increment
of something human
writhing
around a plumb line

lit up like bones inside a fish:

I am alone
it seems to say
but my solitude
knows yours

I kept backing up until it all disappeared
so that near was the same as afar
and nowhere a version of here
and spend was want, grasp was drop,
and to walk was to dribble away

(the thicker I made them
the thinner they got)

what's the meaning
of *here* or *out there*
what does it mean
to say *almost* or *very*?

as if to speak meant
having branches and bearing leaves

as if to leave
meant branching out
and being speechless

"if it's really strong
it will show itself
even if I hide it"

his crushed foot
made the statue limp
right up into the eye of the needle

he was behind its head
he was its pinprick

he took it to a place
where density and zero
were pious friends

he packed the statue in a matchbox
he put a man inside a raindrop
a raindrop without a door
a door without a handle
a handle without a hand

the head grew tiny
and disappeared

disappearance
grew smaller still
until it made a beat
without a heart

not only did they come right up to you
they went right through you
then came back through again
trying to find themselves

and then they remembered
you were
if not their lid
the hinge
on lidlessness

if you make it
you can pull it apart

but the more you take away
the bigger it gets

subtraction
adds up

you aim the vacuum of you
—the vacuum you are
in the plenum you do—
you aim it at you

you *you* you

his eye is a clamp

his studio
an archipelago

for him the line is a man
the man a rotation of skin
at the tip of the brush

or the knife reducing
bodies to dust

each one
less than the next

but more than ever

black and white specks squirming on the screen
the guy next to him watching the movie got
squishy with volume

erasure
seeped out

the street snout was swollen
guzzling its humid sputter of neon

three girls walked into a head
they never noticed was there
but it noticed them

hatching resemblance
from a concave glass

riding their butter
down the slope of shadows

you see that man crossing his legs?
don't stare, but there's no head there

in place of a head
a drizzle of lines
measures the head & heaps it up
heaps it up & dishes it out

every portrait's a pebble
every egg a squall of face
mixed up in the shell

the yolk saw the moon
wipe its promise on a cloud

then the cloud rained men
till it shivered out a dot

the dot undressed
under the trees
into a shudder of dots

the shudder condensed
till a man grew back with a pop

his head was a cloud
but the cloud could shout

from the dollop of his head
the whole dot spills out

its legs grow very long

now they almost reach the ground

unbearable, those
upraised hands
crisp with bones

swarming up
from a terrible roasting

if you can make an image
you can make it breathe

from the opposite shore
he watched it grow
and shrink
at the same time

under the charming smile
the plaster chattered away
and the name of the chatter
was dust

respect the dust

no street
behind no wall

no bulb
emitting light

no grinning scar
no dermal thunder

pumping, where
"Marilyn" "Monroe"

boils over
even if he
moved his hands
upward
around the mass of her clay
over his head? (his head,
where is his head?)

so insatiable
and yet so tacit—

bent over the clay
unswaddling a cry
from the ambient lump
an abyss beckons
from a wet smear

man on stem
head on prong

the same
and the other
and the only

none
and any
and all

triangulate their ardor
like a scream
itching plaster

a face squishes up
from a smudge

a walking finger
opens up space
like the lid of a can

he irrigates the human pouch
the clenched mass
the sack

he puts on the mask
then draws it out like a thread
from the back of his head

the lines of the drawing
swirling in place
excavate a cannibal murmur

of course you know what a head is

you look in the mirror
you bite the mirror
snack on the image

the mirror makes distance
into shadow
shadow into face
to feed a fertilizing
errancy

you have been
where you've never gone
and come back
having not quite
got there yet

yet there you go again

open your eyes
and the object
plunges into your head

a piece of metal
a swish of clay

leaves a lump in your word

advancing and recoiling at once
she pins you to fading

she's almost sexy
except she's a skeleton

her scribble of hips
will whittle you

into a pencil
she will write with

until you are blunt
with extraction

you recede
until you appear
among the missing

where have you gone?
when will being gone
be coming back?

when will being gone
be gone for good?
you prepare

to disappear
if you disappear
your preparation

labors on its own
leaving you behind
in a cowl

of appearance

“I put an apple on my table. Then I put myself into the apple.”
{Je mets une pomme sur ma table. Puis je me mets dans cette pomme.} (Michaux)

How do you tell a story like his? You can’t even get started, so the story ends up being about its own delay, its only and ever present detour into the land of Instead.

Instead of a story, then, a sheaf of immigration papers.

Not only the hands, but the whole man is busy plucking murmurs out of these insensate slivers of clay. His studio competes with dust. The creases in his deeply scored face are depositories of dust. Plaster dust. There are leaks in the roof so it rains indoors, which is why there are so many pots and pans on the floor, to collect the drips; but the buckets leak, the pots have holes, so it rains again. The studio is a constellation of beakers. Everything is on the move, passing through.

His foot was crushed by a car, so he limps. Once, on a trip, his traveling companion, a librarian, died next to him in a hotel room. Another time, he woke up next to a friend after a party only to find the friend dead, cold and dead. These events are elements in a structure, but only if *structure* wanders astray into *invitation*—an invitation addressed to no one, but *he* opened the envelope.

Asked to name the most important encounter of his life, he says: "A white string in a puddle of cold, liquid tar."

Something points, and so it seems to be a hand. The hand swivels in the cage around its exoskeletal spine, or is it a hotel in which you check your bones into a safe deposit vault for the night? Once they've been there, nobody knows what to say about it. This hotel retracts the language from its guests. To be a guest is to be speechless; but at least your bones are safe.

The Pomps of the Subsoils

"What are you digging up?" he asked with alarm.

The story begins with an exhumed puppet, a
miraculated being soaked with tears.
It has huge bulbous eyes, menacing claws, and
below its bared fangs there is, voraciously,
no jaw
—everyone feels a tickling at the heels; the little
ape and the great Achilles alike—
and attached to these jawless lips is a second
mouth, a third, a multitude of mouths,
nostrils, vulvas, nipples.

Your body is with you, though you can't say
how.
You just found yourself with it; you came to
yourself and the world together at once.
Sometimes you suspect it's working even harder
on you than you are on it.
For instance, the body you have may be stored
in a drawer in the morgue.
Smells detonate softly in your memory like
poignant land mines, hidden under the
weedy mass of years and experience.

Your fingers see in the night like cats, gazing
into a black sky where the star of ideas will
rise.
Whether you sit on a park bench or wander
through blooming azaleas, your movements
are not spasmodic reactions to clouds of
atoms, but a lascivious murmur of
hummingbirds blinded by the midday heat.

✠

Between the tip of the brush and the steely gaze,
a volume is born,
pulling and pushing at once, growing and
shrinking, either with or, and with but:
at the end of the body, the mind; but at the end
of the mind, the body.

An atonal logic, at midnight, no longer a thread
unraveled through a maze,
but a simple straight line, bewitching enigma,
this siphon.

A white patch on a white ground: the openly
novel *blank*.
Word responds to word in this gap, as each
builds a humming of its own.

✠

Where does this black sun come from?

This pain and this beauty are linked by their
exactness.

Between us, the glass and I achieve a man.

The Ache of the Exigent

The crinkle of figures on the horizon sputters and goes out.

The mesa exceeds them after all.

In that country all that survives are stooks of lightning you can barely make out through the pounding downpour, the deep gray heave of thunderhead that hung so long on the horizon creamed up ominous overhead abruptly dumping.

Nameless intricate plunge of all possible drops. An hour later the desert sand reappears, shiny, rejuvenated, and already you sense the gritty sputter of grain on dry grain hallucinating a perpetual horizon, saguaro poking up here and there in prickly sponge-barrel tai ch'i postures. And even before

❇

the spliff arrives in Rastaman Vibration the hypnotic jangle of Juno Lewis blown into the conch of *Kulu Se Mama* you feel the sub-thorax ribcage pluckery of mortal strumming in Roslavets' second piano sonata (1916), with a poignant theme of rising notes, as if sniffing the next year's Bolshevik revolution as an expiring sweetness, final resolve of *fin de siècle* longing in peddlepoint. The year before he'd been publishing in a Moscow Futurist journal called *The Vernal Subcontracting Agency of the Muses*. A photo from 1910 shows him bearded, head perched on his left hand is if he's holding a skull that isn't his own; clear penetrating gaze, and long hair clumping over his ears, swept back off the high forehead almost all the way back to Scriabin. Only ten years later, 1920, another photo shows a goateed short-haired man clipped into another era, facing imminent hardships of state-sanctioned culture with less and less use for his polychromatic bunches of tone clusters, "decadent influences" . . . a life eked out in the swelling consequence of the utopia you yearned for, giving you nothing but grief. In 1940, just shy of sixty, after suffering a crippling stroke, Roslavets is finally admitted to the Composer's Union of the USSR.

❄

mechanical repetition

deliberate clumsiness

and prayer

(Paul Griffiths on Stravinsky's
1914 "Three Pieces for String
Quartet")

The Language Homunculus

The Language Homunculus "perceives" the
world through hundreds of censors
connected to various parts of the reactor.
She can identify consciousness, not just
organisms or entities in general.
Modifying loose connections in the monitor is
called Biology.
The Language Homunculus is allowed to impose
deletion rules in accordance with the
"Average Language Homunculus" or the
"Turbulent Inner Language Homunculus."
But now imagine what it would be like to follow
the behavior of The Language
Homunculus and understand it.
Rules will be generated out of "thin air."
Hypotheses will be formulated and deleted "at
whim."

We can understand the cardinal instincts of The
Language Homunculus
without appealing to her *When* or *Where*, *Howl*
or *Whine:*
nothing can stand in the way of her Desire
for *she is a Queen, and she is a
Nature Machine.*

She can borrow a book.
She can walk and feign weariness.
She can gleam or glisten in the shadowy pool.
For she is boundless white and plunging, or tiny
twisted columns of moonshine from a
flying temple crowded with rain.
Newts crawl like tiny dragons past her drinking
bees, who economize wingbeats to the
limit.
She is instinct sodden with blackberry bloom.
She is a Garden of Eden blackboard on which
erasing is taking place.

Rectifying the Eventual

> The adventure of a family of kangaroos, of course, is an extremely clear example of a comic interpretation of the formula of ecstasy. (Sergei Eisenstein)

that was then
this is now

as now now
as it was then

when then
was a former now

known in nouns
and sometimes verbs

as if "y" and "sometimes w"
were vowels, & vowels were owls

*

the string navigates itself into a contortion
and then the shoe is tied

if you can't persuade the string to do it
you'll have to do it yourself

*

the paper clip of cognition
still springs eternal in the out box

where the next you
denudes the me that used to be

(I used to be you, you know
but got used to being me instead

until nothing was left
but density & snag)

*

a door ajar
a tooth or two
a smiling faucet
& all at once
the mind is like a clown act

comparing a cow with a worm
a norm with an arm
an absolute
with modesty or crumbs

meanwhile
a piece of meat tries to make the scene

two drops of saliva go down the street
fetching the arrow of time
from the quiver of space

&

suddenly there you are
all night long
stooped over the burner
steaming the postage stamp of the concept
off the envelope of representation
watching words bubble up
to captivate experience

*

there's a mountain of pacing about
that wears a trench of you
down to sprung plush
gulp on gulp

there's also a mountain
of meaningless Hercules
where dowel pins owl
hour by horrible hour

there's an estuary

where meaning doesn't mix
with matter —what's the matter
with that estuary? what's it mean?

instead of beginning, middle & end:
beginning the middle again
& again, end to end

as though As If were a cage
in which birds were stuck to the sky
& feathers were weather

*

ooooooh, looky here
here's an experimental flesh they want you to
wear
so you don't wake up
you wake *down*

wondering
what did god the goad   learn to think
          to make matter   talk back with?

Mr. Blank is out there *Bossing the Universe*
                    on your behalf

this is it, Land of the Knowing Look:
everywhere you go
the fecund minimum

stares you down

so there must be a “self” that correlates to all
this
rubble of experience
[—shall I (de)posit one?]

what’s up? what’s down? & *what’s it to you ?*

does the hound of the Baskervilles bark at the
Owl of Minerva?

Let’s have that again, does the... No,
never you mind.

A sentence and a worm are *stupid animals.*
The dusk is in *French.*
Danger is *one new word.*
A rap on the door is an index.
Why do *cinders* grumble?
Call it The Average Itch of the Phantom Rider.
The ball gown reverts to mystical mud.
No universal ego, just an *ash-pit.*

It’s only a technical maelstrom, so let it go.

Doctor Because might know who you are.
Let’s give him a ring, shall we?

His feet are webbed, his neck is long,
his iridescent demeanor will astound you.

He's the sole survivor of four of his kind.
But he's not what you think.

His intentions suffuse you with gravity
and yet you float. His happy children
smear about like a slick paste
until dawn breaks.

He is used to you by now.
His pivot is a legend
raised on happy food.

Bring me a glass of water
he says to the spark.

Like an oiled axle
he shines in the watery light.

He's a bubble
pleading at your door.

*

Or is it pulling?
Pulling or purring
it purrs. He purrs.
It's a person

enabled to appear:
a fast poison singular
relieving itself
in the dis-
continuous ex-
tremities
of the subject.

*

It would have been a zero day in County
Whiteout
a squirrel imploded with the force of a bull
or was it you?
& if I wonder was it you
do you wonder it too?

It was a very old hour in the math of afternoon
a kangaroo peaceably bullies an owl
it will be a very old owl

I was an odd duck, wasn't I
but where was I sitting?

He could move a ballerina with his mountain
to make ends meet
until someone blinks first
then yesterday is over

It might as well be a day off

to hear you tell it:
what else did you tell it to do?
"Go home, little mouse," the bayonet says
to the friend or maybe cousin of the voice
voiceless in an anecdote
the speech therapist knows
who gives you measles over the phone

which is not at all the same as saying
less & less of the same thing over & over
until less is more, more or less, unless you let
that
cat out of the bag, & more and more of "less is
more"
is more than you can take—& what's more,
it's there for the taking

("take it or leave it
 but where does taking it leave it?")

how else would you know
what Mr. Sugar does after dark

but it's still a neat trick how it all came back
tomorrow

Pollock's Hectic Pigment

begins with a vertebral column, or is it a pile of
radiating eyes?

What if you scratch the word *Fire* until you get
Untitled (Overall Composition)—the title's
untitled?

A coiled snake composes a cranial puddle—
gurgles down the last of the Jungian
symbols with an anamorphic squawk.

The pouring begins as a drizzle of effacements,
but will that pyramidal eye still pick its way
among the dribbled arteries of a new
ordinance?

Guardians of the Secret: a hot capillary pucker of
eyes in the chest, the incipient drip *is* the
secret of the insistent quadrant and the
guardians are what? a splash gathering in
the wrist, or the impulsive spectacle?

What could have been Moby-Dick shudders into
Pasiphaë, with a click or thud of coupling
trains; everything sifts into the possible all

at once: here's a knuckle, an ankle, a wrist,
three blue udders and a nostril nearby, a
zigzag where once was a mind, a smear
begetting the consummate.

Postwar means a dirty flash of Matisse, or does
the slumped oval make this one Gothic?
What does the intimate blue begrudge?
What does a pulse confounding a bone *do*?
In this vista of heckled complicity, what is
this protest, this pause that means figures
are bound to emerge?

Free Form says *Take Me, I'm Yours*—no
form's free, but freed *into* the next, like a
glass eye searing the artery as it noses up
into your heart.

These could be aerial recon photos of bombed
out cities.

This web of *Phosphorescence* is how we are
made, made of the comet, the blue thrall,
the middle plummet coveting bottom and
top, inside and out all at once. Blue can be
your aperture here. Fat "A" crouches in
another *Untitled*. Sometimes lines come and
go from a mouth—leak and wander—
sometimes a squiggle reverts to a medical

chart: its transparencies are pull-away skins
of an etch-a-sketch mystic writing pad.

Now we come into the country we know—
spider arabesque. Grim tutorials of chance
subsiding in a spellbound squeal,
Queequeg's casket itching with hieroglyphs
inside and out till it's all inside-out. A tattoo
of dunk. Eye chowder. Shudder and chatter.
What is embellishment now? He's clipped a
figure from a different blur and pasted it
over the stars until there's a snout of
dangling silhouettes, almost a waddle that
wants to say it can't dance. But does.

Posture is also a drip. What's over, what's
under? What's up, what's down?

The cut-outs are guzzling glass and nails (the
better to see you with, my dear). A skittish
red; and the wiggle of the puddle makes
pastoral queasy, filtered through this
arterial perimeter where coagulates relent,
and the winter's tale like a glazed saucer's
beginning to crack. Every gazing face a
fissure, a droplet of pigments gathering
clots from the smear. Everything is big, and
yet the tiny secrecy of lineation shudders
with intensity. Rapture on a floor daubed up
as *bent*. A gob of yellow pregnant with a

white swirl. Scarlet veins a soluble distress. When at last a figure appears, an ossuary is near. Something's likely to be bones. Puffs are symptoms, narcotic flagellants. Some of the smudges are birds and they fly away. *Number 23* is a musical note. Though there, as ever, is the gaping mouth.

Altamira chirps hello in *1A*. And in 1953 there's that eye again, lurking in the triangle. *The Deep* is trying to be milked. *White Light*. All a gape, and again. All this "hectic pigment" magnifies the bone deposits, wouldn't you say? From drizzle to dazzle to drunk and dead, the unconscious paraded is boiling up a serum. Humbled and assessed is how these paintings make you feel, their *light* in which you appear, then disappear.

Jed Rasula's previous collections of poetry include *Tabula Rasula* (1986) and *Hot Wax, or Psyche's Drip* (2007). He co-edited *Imagining Language* (1998) with Steve McCaffery, and *Burning City: Poems of Metropolitan Modernity* (2012) with Tim Conley. Currently a professor at the University of Georgia, Rasula has worked in radio, television, publishing, and other trades.

www.ingramcontent.com/pod-product-compliance
Lightning Source LLC
Chambersburg PA
CBHW052136010526
44113CB00036B/2284
* 9 7 8 0 9 9 7 3 0 4 8 2 4 *